SCOTTISH
COUNTRY RECIPES

COMPILED BY
PIPPA GOMAR & MOLLY PERHAM

COUNTY PUBLICATIONS

Maidstone

SCOTLAND

Scotland is a rugged country with little more than a quarter of the land under cultivation. The soil is poorer than in England and the weather wetter and colder. In early times the mainstay of the Scottish peasant's diet used to be oats and barley, which grow well in the inhospitable climate. Every cottage had its own girnel, or oatmeal barrel, and oakcakes or bannocks were cooked on an iron bakestone over a peat fire. This method of cooking was used well into the last century in some of the Scottish Islands. For the modern Scottish housewife baked food still remains an important part of the diet, from freshly-baked morning rolls, or baps, to the substantial array of cakes, scones, gingerbread and shortbreads that are served for the favourite meal of the day – high tea.

Oats and barley were augmented by kail and by vegetables and fruits that grew wild in the hedgerows – raspberries, strawberries, gooseberries, blaeberries, wild spinach, carrots and nettles. The kail-pot was also made of iron – it was a large round cauldron with a lid and three legs that stood over the fire. Soups and broths, often substantial enough to be a meal on their own, were made from any available vegetables and bones of game, rabbit, meat of fish. The potato was introduced from Ireland in the 18th century, and at about that time knowledge of crop husbandry and improved methods of agriculture began to be used so that more varied vegetables were grown.

The uncultivated areas of Scotland, particularly in the North and West, are famous for their game. The rolling moorlands are home to red grouse, ptarmigan, blackcock, capercaillie, partridge, wild duck, pheasant, woodcock and snipe. Deer roam in the Highland forests.

The Scots have never eaten much pork, but Scottish beef and

lamb have gained fame throughout the world. Traditional beef breeds include the Aberdeen Angus, the Galloway and the Highland. Cheviots and Shetlands are the most popular breeds of sheep.

The sheep and beef cattle graze on the uplands, while the lowlands provide rich pastureland for the dairy herds. The county of Ayrshire has given its name to a breed of cattle developed there that has become popular throughout Great Britain because of its high milk yield. Being high in butterfat, the milk is ideal for making cheese like Highland Soft. Dunlop, a hard cheese, is also made in this part of Scotland, as well as on the Orkneys, Arran and Islay. Scottish Cheddar is produced in creameries in the uplands.

Crowdie, an old Highland cheese, is made by souring milk naturally in the sun. The cream is then skimmed off for butter, and the thickened milk 'scrambled' on the stove to make the whey drain off. The resulting curds are wrapped in muslin and left to drain. Served with oatcakes, crowdie had been eaten in the Highlands and Islands since the days of the Picts.

Fishing is an important Scottish industry, and has been so since the eleventh century. Until then, the Celtic Church has forbidden fish to be used as a food. Inland, the rivers of Scotland are stacked with salmon and trout, while huge catches of herring are landed at Aberdeen, and because they are so plentiful and cheap they have always been an important part of the Scottish diet – cooked in a large pot with tatties (potatoes) or fried in a coating of oatmeal. Those that were not consumed by the local people were preserved by salting and smoking. Scotch herring are ideal for kippers because they are large and have a high fat content. Loch Fyne remains the centre of the kipper trade.

Other fish caught off Scottish shores are haddock, cod, mackerel, halibut, sole and plaice. Finnan haddock is a particular delicacy that originated in the village of Findon near Aberdeen. Smokies, or 'pinwiddies' are small haddock that have been hot-smoked, and these come from the tiny hamlet of Auchmithie near Arbroath.

Scottish traditional cuisine tends to be heavy and filling to satisfy the appetites of men who have spent a day out in the cold. But it also owes a rather more delicate touch to the influence of the French, who came and went during the period of the Auld Alliance in the 16th century. James V of Scotland married a French noblewoman, Mary of Lorraine, and entertaining in the French manner became the rage amongst the aristocracy. The French influence is still evident in some of the recipes and culinary terms, but good, plain, wholesome food is what the country has always been, and still is, famous for.

Fair fa' your honest, sonsie face,
Great chieftain o' the puddin'-race
Aboon them a' ye tak your place,
Painch, tripe, or thairm :
Weel are ye wordy o' a grace
As lang's my arm.

From *To a Haggis* by Robert Burns.

RECIPES

SCONES and GIRDLE CAKES

BREAD

SUNDRIES

PRESERVES

SWEETS

DRINKS

HIGHLAND GAME SOUP

Serves 6-8

This rich, clear soup from the Highlands of Scotland can be made with left-over trimmings and carcasses from any type of game – grouse, pheasant or partridge; rabbit, hare or venison.

Left-over trimmings and carcasses of game
1 onion
1 carrot
1 blade of mace
1 bay leaf
3 cloves
2 sprigs of parsley
2 pints (1.15 litres) beef stock
Salt and pepper
1 oz (25 g) lean beef
1 glass Marsala or sherry

Put the left-over trimmings and carcasses into a large saucepan.

Add the peeled and sliced onion and carrot, the mace, bay leaf, cloves and parsley.

Pour over the beef stock.

Season with salt and pepper.

Bring to the boil.

Skim off any scum that rises to the surface.

Simmer for two hours, then strain.

Return the soup to the saucepan and add the beef, coarsley chopped.

Bring to the boil again and strain.

Add the Marsala or sherry and reheat before serving.

SCOTCH BROTH

Serves 6-8

This soup is so nourishing and filling that it is a meal in itself. It has always been popular with farming families.

1 lb (450 g) neck of mutton
4 pints (2.25 litres) cold water
2 oz (50 g) pearl barley, washed
2 oz (50 g) dried peas, soaked overnight
2 carrots
2 leeks
1 small turnip
1 onion
1 stick celery
Salt and pepper
Half a small cabbage, shredded
A sprig of parsley

Put the meat into a large saucepan.

Cover with cold water.

Add the salt, pearl barley, and peas.

Bring to the boil.

Skim off any scum that rises to the surface.

Dice the carrots, leeks, turnip, onion and celery and add to the pan.

Season with salt and pepper.

Bring to the boil, cover, and simmer for $2^{1/2}$ hours.

Add the shredded cabbage and cook for a further 20 minutes.

Adjust the seasoning.

Garnish with the chopped parsley before serving.

COCK-A-LEEKIE

This is traditionally served as the first course on Hogmanay or at a Burn's Supper. The Scots so love their national soup that many odes have been written to it.

> 'Lang may ye live, an' lang enjoy
> Ilk blessin' life can gie,
> Health, wealth, content and pleasure,
> An' cock-a-leekie.'

1 boiling fowl, with giblets
4 pints (2.25 litres) cold water
6 shredded leeks
2 tablespoons rice
1 tablespoon chopped parsley
Salt and pepper to taste

Place the fowl and giblets in a large saucepan and cover with cold water.

Bring to the boil. Skim off any scum.

Simmer gently for 2 hours, skimming again of necessary.

Add the shredded leeks and rice and simmer for a further hour.

Remove the bird and giblets from the soup.

Add the chopped parsley. Season to taste.

The chicken meat can be served as a separate course.

HOTCH POTCH

Also called Hairst Bree, meaning harvest broth, this soup-stew was made in the summer when all the vegetables were young and crisp. The freshness of the vegetables gives the soup its sweet flavour.

> 'Then here's to ilka kindly Scot:
> Wi' mony gude broths he boils his pot,
> But rare hotch-potch beats a' the lot,
> It smells and smacks sae brawly.'

> Sheriff Bell

8 oz (225 g) neck of lamb
2 pints (1.15 litres) water
Salt and pepper
3 fresh young carrots
2 fresh young turnips
1/2 small cauliflower
1 onion (or 4 spring onions)
4 oz (100 g) broad beans
4 oz (100 g) shelled peas
4 leaves of lettuce or cabbage
1 level teaspoon sugar
1 tablespoon chopped parsley

Put the meat into a saucepan and cover with the cold water.

Season with salt and pepper.

Bring to the boil.

Skim off any scum that rises to the surface.

Simmer gently for 1 1/2 hours.

Dice the carrots and turnips.

Divide the cauliflower into small sprigs.

Peel and slice the onion or spring onions.

Add these and the broad beans to the saucepan and simmer for a further 30-40 minutes.

Add the shelled peas and shredded lettuce or cabbage leaves and simmer for a further 10 minutes.

Remove the meat and cut it into small dice.

Return to the pan.

Add the sugar and chopped parsley.

Check the seasoning.

Serve hot.

LENTIL BRO

Serves 8-10

This soup comes from the Shetland Islands.

2 oz (50 g) butter
8 oz (225 g) lentils
2 oz (50 g) barley
1 large onion, finely chopped
1 carrot, diced
2 sticks of celery, chopped
1/2 small turnip, diced
Salt and pepper
4 pints (2.25 litres) ham stock
Chopped parsley for garnishing

Melt the butter in a large saucepan.

Add the lentils, barley, and prepared vegetables.

Season with salt and pepper.

Cook gently for 10 minutes, stirring occasionally.

Add the stock.

Bring to the boil and simmer for $1^{1/2}$-2 hours.

Check the seasoning.

Serve hot, garnish with chopped parsley.

CULLEN SKINK

This is a traditional fisherman's soup from the North East of Scotland. It should be made with a true Finnan-haddie – a Finnan haddock that has been lightly smoked but not dyed. Skink is an old Scots word for soup or broth.

1 large smoked Finnan haddock
1 onion, chopped
1/2 pint (300 ml/1$^{1/2}$ cups) water
Salt and pepper
1 pint (600 ml/2$^{1/2}$ cups) milk
1 oz (25 g) butter
1/2 lb (225 g) mashed potato

Put the haddock and chopped onion into a saucepan and cover with water.

Bring to the boil and simmer for about 15 minutes, until the flesh comes away from the bone.

Put the flesh to one side.

Put the skin and bones back into the pan.

Season with salt and pepper.

Cook for a further hour.

Strain the fish stock and discard the skin and bones.

Add the flaked flesh, milk, butter and mashed potato to the fish stock.

Bring back to the boil and simmer for a few minutes.

Serve hot.

HERRINGS IN OATMEAL

Serves 4

4 large herrings
Salt and pepper
4 oz (100 g) oatmeal
2 oz (50 g) butter
1 tablespoon oil
Lemon to garnish

Wash and gut the herrings.

Split them.

Run the blade of a knife down the backbone, pressing firmly, and lift it out.

Sprinkle the herrings with salt and pepper.

Dip the fish in the oatmeal, pressing it well in until they are well coated.

Heat the butter and oil in a frying pan, but do not allow the pan to get too hot, or the oatmeal will burn and the fish become too dry.

Fry the herrings, split side down, for about 4 minutes or until well browned.

Turn and fry the other side until brown and crisp.

Drain on kitchen paper.

Garnish with lemon wedges.

FINNAN HADDOCK

The Finnan, or Findon, haddock takes its name from a village in Kincardineshire. It is split and cleaned before curing, and is a golden yellow colour with a nutty flavour. Finnan haddocks may be grilled, steamed, or poached.

To grill : Brush each haddock with melted butter and grill lightly on both sides. Top each haddock with two lightly poached eggs.

To steam : Cut each haddock lengthwise, then across. Place in a saucepan with enough water to cover. Add a rasher of bacon. Cover with a close-fitting lid and steam for 5 minutes.

To poach : Cut each haddock in half down the middle. Put into a large saucepan and cover with boiling water. Simmer gently for 5 minutes. Drain off the water.

To make a sauce for poached Finnan haddock :

1/2 oz (15 g) butter
1 teaspoon cornflour
1/2 pint (300 ml/1$^{1/4}$ cups) milk
Salt and pepper
1 hard-boiled egg
1 teaspoon chopped parsley

Melt the butter in a small saucepan.

Cream the cornflour with a little of the milk.

Add to the melted butter.

Stir in the remainder of the milk.

Bring to the boil, stirring all the time.

Season with salt and pepper.

Pour over the fish.

Chop the hard-boiled egg and sprinkle on top

Garnish with chopped parsley.

CRAPPIT HEIDS

Serves 4

This recipe comes from the Hebrides, and is a way of using up the liver from white fish. The liver melts away into the oatmeal when it is cooked, and the bones from the head and flavour. The Scots word 'crap' means to stuff or fill.

4 large haddock heads
4 haddock livers
Oatmeal
Salt and pepper
Milk to bind

Clean the fish heads thoroughly.

Place the fish livers in a bowl and cover with cold water.

Add some salt and soak for 1 hour.

Strain.

Chop the livers and mix with an equal quantity of oatmeal.

Season with salt and pepper.

Moisten with a little milk.

Stuff the haddock heads loosely with the filling, leaving room for the oatmeal to swell.

Tie securely with thread.

Wrap in foil and put into a pan of boiling water.

Simmer for 30 minutes.

Serve the heads on their own or with portions of plain boiled fish.

GRILLED MACKEREL WITH GOOSEBERRY SAUCE

Serves 4

The sharp flavour of a gooseberry sauce goes well with the oiliness of mackerel.

4 medium mackerel
A little melted butter
Salt and pepper

For the sauce :
8 oz (225 g) gooseberries
1/2 oz (15 g) butter
1 oz (25 g) sugar
A pinch of ground nutmeg
1 teaspoon lemon juice
Salt and pepper

Ask the fishmonger to gut the mackerel.

Wash the fish thoroughly and with a sharp knife make three diagonal scores on each side.

Brush with melted butter.

Sprinkle with salt and pepper.

Put the mackerel into a buttered grill pan and grill slowly for about 10 minutes on each side.

To make the sauce :

Top and tail the gooseberries and wash them.

Put into a saucepan with the butter and cook gently to a soft pulp.

Rub the fruit through a sieve.

Stir in the sugar, nutmeg, lemon juice, and a little salt and pepper.

Serve with the grilled mackerel.

NEWHAVEN CREAM

This baked fish pudding gets its name from an old fishing village near Edinburgh. It may also be steamed in a bowl for about 1$^{1/2}$ hours, instead of baking in the oven.

1 lb (450 g) Aberdeen fish fillet
1/2 pint (300 ml/1$^{1/4}$ cups) milk
2 oz (50 g) melted butter
3 oz (75 g) fresh white breadcrumbs
2 tablespoons chopped parsley
3 eggs
1/4 pint (150 ml/2/3 cup) cream
Salt and pepper

For the sauce :
1/4 pint (150 ml/2/3 cup) milk
1/2 oz (15 g) butter
1/2 oz (15 g) flour
1 tablespoon chopped parsley

Put the fish into a saucepan. Pour over the milk.

Bring to the boil, cover and simmer for 5 minutes.

Skin and flake the fish. Reserve the cooking liquid.

Put the melted butter, breadcrumbs, parsley, eggs and cream into a bowl and add the fish.

Mix together thoroughly. Season with salt and pepper.

Pour into a greased 2 pint (1 litre) soufflé mould.

Cover with greaseproof paper or foil.

Set the dish in a tin containing about 1 inch (2.5 cm) water and bake in a moderate oven for 30 minutes.

To make the sauce :
Melt the butter in a small saucepan and add the flour.

Cook gently for a couple of minutes, then gradually add the milk, stirring all the time to prevent lumps.

Bring to the boil so that the sauce thickens.

Season and add the parsley.

To serve :
Turn the fish pudding out on to a warm serving dish and pour over the sauce. Serve hot.

Oven : 350°F/180°C   Gas Mark 4

TROUT WITH ALMONDS

Serves 4

4 rainbow trout
1 oz (25 g) seasoned flour
3 oz (75 g) butter
1 tablespoon corn oil
2 oz (50 g) flaked almonds
Juice of half a lemon

Clean the fish but leave the heads on.

Wash and dry the fish thoroughly.

Toss in the seasoned flour.

Melt 1 oz (25 g) of the butter and the oil in a frying pan.

Fry the fish two at a time for 5 minutes on each side.

Drain and keep warm on a serving dish.

Wipe the frying pan clean and melt the rest of the butter.

Fry the almonds until they are brown.

Remove the pan from the heat and stir in the lemon juice.

Spoon the almond mixture over the fish and serve.

TWEED KETTLE

Serves 6

The Tweed is one of the great salmon rivers of Scotland. The recipe comes from Edinburgh.

2 lbs (900 g) fresh salmon
2 spring onions, finely chopped
A pinch of mace
1/4 pint (150 ml/2/3 cup) dry white wine
Salt and pepper
1 oz (25 g) butter
4 oz (100 g) mushrooms
1 tablespoon chopped parsley

Put the salmon into a fish kettle or large pan and cover with water.

Bring to the boil, simmer gently for 3 minutes.

Remove the skin from the salmon and take out all the bones.

Cut the flesh into small cubes.

Return the skin and bones to the cooking liquid, bring to the boil and simmer for 15 minutes.

Strain and pour off 1/4 pint (150 ml/2/3 cup) into a clean saucepan.

Add the cubed fish, chopped spring onions, mace, and white wine.

Season with salt and pepper.

Cover and simmer gently for 10 minutes.

Melt the butter in another saucepan.

Chop the mushrooms into small pieces and cook them gently in the butter.

Drain, and add to the salmon mixture.

Continue cooking the mixture for a further 5 minutes. Turn out on to a serving dish, garnish with chopped parsley.

ROAST PHEASANT

Serves 6

The pheasant season is from 1st October to 1st February, and they are in prime condition in November and December. Pheasant are often bought by the brace – which means a cock and a hen bird. The cock usually weighs 3-3$^{1/4}$ lb (1.5-1.6 kg), and the hen bird about 2-2$^{1/2}$ lb (1-1.5 kg). The hen bird usually has more flavour and is less dry than tle cock. Birds should be hung for at least ten days.

A brace of pheasant
6 oz (175 g) fresh white breadcrumbs
4 oz (100 g) melted butter
4 rashers of streaky bacon
Watercress for garnish

Wipe the birds inside and out.

Stir the breadcrumbs into the melted butter.

Divide the stuffing mixture into two and spoon into the carcass of each bird.

Truss the birds and place in a roasting tin.

Lay two rashers of bacon over the breast of each bird.

Roast in a hot oven for 10 minutes, then reduce the heat and cook for a further 45 minutes.

Ten minutes before the end of cooking time remove the bacon so that the breasts can brown.

Arrange the roast birds on a serving dish and garnish with watercress.

Serve with game chips and bread sauce.

Oven : 425°F/220°C   Gas Mark 7

Reduce to : 350°F/180°C   Gas Mark 4

PIGEON CASSEROLE

Serves 4

During the 19th century most large houses had a dovecot and pigeons were a source of extra meat.

2 pigeons
1 oz (25 g) butter
1 tablespoon cooking oil
4 oz (100 g) streaky bacon
2 onions, peeled and sliced
1/2 pint (300 ml/1¼ cups) tomato juice
1/2 pint (300 ml/1¼ cups) chicken stock
A bouquet garni
Salt and pepper
2 slices white bread
A little lard

Wipe the pigeons, and cut each one in half along the breast and backbone.

Heat the butter and oil in a frying pan until smoking hot and brown the pigeon pieces all over.

Transfer to a casserole dish.

Cut the bacon into pieces and fry with the onion in the remaining fat. Transfer to a casserole dish.

Pour over the tomato juice and stock, add the bouquet garni, and season with salt and pepper.

Cover the casserole and bake in a moderately hot oven for 2 hours, or until the meat is tender.

Near the end of cooking time cut the crusts off the bread and cut each slice into four triangles.

Heat the lard in a frying pan and fry the pieces of bread until they are golden brown on each side.

Remove the casserole from the oven, take out the bouquet garni and scatter the triangles of bread over the surface.

Oven : 375°F/190°C   Gas Mark 5

CIVET OF VENISON

Serves 6

1¹/² lbs (675 g) venison
2 rashers of bacon
Seasoned flour
1 oz (25 g) lard
1 oz (25 g) flour
1 tablespoon wine vinegar
1 glass red wine or port
1/4 pint (150 ml/2/3 cup) stock
2 onions, sliced
2 oz (50 g) mushrooms, sliced
Pepper

Cut the venison meat into cubes.

Remove the rind from the bacon and cut into pieces.

Toss the venison and bacon in seasoned flour.

Melt the lard in a large saucepan and fry the venison and bacon until brown all over.

Sprinkle over the flour, stir, and cook gently for 2 minutes.

Gradually add the vinegar, red wine, and stock, stirring all the time to prevent lumps.

Add the sliced onions.

Season with pepper to taste.

Cover with a well-fitting lid and simmer for 2-2¹/² hours until tender.

Add the sliced mushrooms 30 minutes before the end of cooking time.

HAGGIS

Haggis is generally considered to be the national dish of Scotland. It is a simple, frugal meal using those parts of an animal that might otherwise be discarded, mixed with oats and seasoning.

Haggis is eaten throughout the year, but particularly on Hogmanay (31 December) and on Burns' Night (25 January). At Burns' suppers an elaborate ritual called the 'Ceremony of the Piping of the Haggis' is performed. The Haggis is carried in on a silver platter to the sound of bagpipes. While the host quotes Burns' *Address to a Haggis,* it is slashed open with a *skein dhu*, the small dagger traditionally worn in the Scotsman's knee-length sock. The haggis is then piped back to the kitchen, where it is dished out with chappit tatties and bashed neeps (hot mashed potatoes and swedes). It is usual to serve small glasses of neat whisky with the haggis - this is sipped in between mouthfuls, or poured over the haggis.

The stomach bag and pluck (heart, liver and lights) of a sheep
3 onions
1 lb (450 g) pinhead oatmeal
8 oz (225 g) shreddes suet
Salt and pepper

Wash the stomach bag thoroughly in cold water.
Turn it inside out and scald it.
Scrape the surface with a knife.
Soak overnight in cod salted water.
Next day wash the pluck (heart, liver and lights) and put them into a pan of boiling water, letting the windpipe hang over the side.
Add a teaspoon of salt.
Boil for 2 hours.
Remove the pluck from the pan and cut away the windpipe and any gristle.
Parboil the onions, drain then them and reserve the water.
Chop the onions thoroughly.
Toast the pinhead oatmeal until golden brown.
Mince half the liver with all the heart and lights.
Stir in the chopped onions, toasted oatmeal and shredded suet.
Season well with salt and peper.
Add enough of the water from boiling the onions to make a soft mixture.
With the rough surface of the stomach bag on the outside, fill it three-quarters full with the mixture - room must be left for the oatmeal to swell.
Sew the bag up with a trussing needle using coarse thread or very fine tring.

Prick the bag here and there with the needle.

Place the haggis on an old enamel plate and put it into a pan of boiling water.

Cover the pan and simmer slowly for 3 hours, adding more water if necessary to keep the haggis covered.

When cooked, remove the pan and place on a warmed plate.

Remove the threads and slit open the bag.

Serve piping hot, with mashed potatoes, swedes and plenty of butter.

HIGHLAND BEEF BALLS
Serves 3-4

These beef balls should be highly flavoured, but the spices suggested may be varied according to taste.

1 lb (450 g) minced meat
2 oz (50 g) suet
1/2 teaspoon ginger
1/2 teaspoon mace
1/2 teaspoon ground cloves
1/2 teaspoon dark brown sugar
Salt and pepper
1 egg, beaten
Medium oatmeal to coat
Oil for deep-frying

Mix the minced beef thoroughly with the suet, spices adn sugar.

Bind together with the beaten egg.

Divide the mixture into six or eight equal-sized pieces and roll into balls.

Coat the balls in oatmeal.

Deep-fry for 5 - 7 minutes until the balls are a deep brown colour.

SCOTCH BRAISED BEEF

Serves 4-6

1 1/2 lb (675 g) topside of beef
4 oz (100 g) streaky bacon
1 carrot
1 stick of celery
1 small turnip
1 small onion
1 oz (25 g) butter
4 allspice berries
10 peppercorns
1 blade mace
1 sprig marjoram
A sprig of parsley
Salt and pepper
1 1/2 pints (900 ml/ 3 3/4 cups) stock
1 oz (25 g) cornflour

Remove the rind from the bacon and cut into small pieces.

Dice the vegetables.

Melt the butter in a deep saucepan.

When smoking hot, add the bacon and vegetables and fry for 5 minutes, stirring frequently.

Remove the bacon and vegetables from the pan and fry the beef on all sides until it is browned and the juices are sealed in .

Put the bacon and vegetables back into the saucepan around the beef.

Tie the herbs into a muslin bag and add to the pan.

Season with salt and pepper.

Pour in the stock and bring to the boil.

Cover with the lid and simmer gently for 2 - 2 1/2 hours, or until the meat is tender.

Lift the meat out on to a serving dish.

Remove the herb bag.

Mix the cornflour with a little cold water to a thin paste and stir into the stock

Arrange the vegetables around the meat with a little of the gravy.

Serve the rest of the gravy in a sauceboat.

SCOTCH COLLOPS   Serves 4

1 lb (450 g) minced meat
1 oz (25 g) beef dripping
1 large onion
1 carrot
1/2 pint (300 ml/ 1¼ cups) stock
1 tablespoon oatmeal
Salt and peper

Melt the dripping in a saucepan until it is smoking hot.

Put in the mince and allow to seal.

Cook until nicely browned all over.

Dice the onion and carrot and add to the meat.

Add the stock and oatmeal.

Season well with salt and pepper.

Allow to simmer slowly for about an hour until the mince is cooked and most of the liquid evaporated.

Serve with hot mashed potatoes and swedes.

ABERDEEN SAUSAGE

This is an old farmhouse recipe for using up the end of a ham. if you use half pork instead of all beef this makes a more moist sausage. The sausage may be steamed or baked. Serve it cold with potato salad and baby beetroots.

1 lb (450 g) stewing beef
** (or 8 oz (225 g) beef and 8 oz (225 g) shoulder of pork)**
12 oz (350 g) streaky bacon
1 onion
4 oz (100 g) rolled oats
6 fresh leaves, finely chopped
A pinch of grated nutmeg
Salt and pepper
Browned breadcrumbs

Mince the beef (or beef and pork), bacon and onion.

Mix in the rolled oats, sage and nutmeg. Season well. Bind the mixture together with the beaten egg.

For the steaming method:

Mould the mixture into a sausage shape and wrap in greaseproof paper. Scald a pudding cloth and wrap the sausage in it, tying securely at the ends.

Bring a large pan of water to the boil and lower the sausage into it, peferably resting on a heatproof plate.

Cover, and simmer gently for 3 hours.

When cooked, remove the pudding cloth and greaseproof paper.

Roll in browned breadcrumbs while still hot.

For the baking method:

Press the sausage mixture into a greased ovenproof dish.

Cover with buttered greaseproof paper and then foil.

Stand the dish in a roasting tin and pour boiling water round it. Bake in a moderate oven for 2 hours

When cooked, remove the foil and greaseproof paper and pour in a little hot stock.

Cover again with foil and put a weight on top to keep it firm.

Leave overnight.

Next day, turn out the cooked sausage and coat well with browned breadcrumbs.

Oven: 350°F/180°C   Gas Mark 4.

ABERDEEN MEAT ROLL   Serves 4

12 oz (375 g) lean steak mince
6 oz (175 g) streaky unsmoked bacon (minced)
1 beaten egg
4 tablespoons water
A little freshly ground black pepper
4 oz (100 g) fresh breadcrumbs
Extra breadcrumbs for coating

Mix together the steak mince, the minced bacon and breadcrumbs. Season with freshly ground pepper.

Add the beaten egg and the water and stir to combine well.

Turn the mixture into a greased pudding basin, cover with greaseproof paper and tie down with string.

Put the pudding basin into a saucepan half filled with boiling water. Cover and steam for 2 hours.

Leave to cool slightly.

Turn the meat roll out and roll in the extra breadcrumbs.

Serve cold.

ROYAL GAME PIE

Serves 6

1 pheasant
Seasoned flour
6 oz (175 g) mushrooms
1 large onion
4 rashers of streaky bacon
1 tablespoon chopped parsley
A pinch of dried mixed herbs
1/4 pint (150 ml/2/3 cup) stock
1/4 pint (150 ml/2/3 cup) red wine or port
Salt and pepper
8 oz (225 g) puff pastry
Milk or beaten egg to glaze

Joint the pheasant.

Toss the pieces in the seasoned flour.

Arrange in a 2$^{1/2}$ pint (1.5 litre) pie dish.

Slice the mushrooms, and peel and slice the onion.

Remove the rind from the bacon and chop into small pieces.

Add the mushrooms, onion and bacon to the pie dish.

Add the chopped parsley and herbs.

Pour over the stock and wine.

Season well with salt and pepper.

Roll out the pastry to make a lid to fit the pie dish, sealing it down with a little water.

Use any trimmings to make pastry leaves to decorate the pie.

Brush with milk or beaten egg to glaze.

Bake in a hot oven for 20 minutes, then reduce the heat and bake for a further 2 hours.

If necessary, cover the pie with greaseproof paper to stop the pastry from burning.

Oven: 425°F/220°C   Gas Mark 7

Reduce to: 325°F/160°C   Gas Mark 3.

VEAL PIE

Serves 4

This dish dates back to the Auld Alliance with France. To make it really extravagant a chopped truffle can be added.

A veal cutlets
1/2 teaspoon dried herbs
A pinch of ground mace
Salt and pepper
8 rashers of streaky bacon
2 boiled egg yolks or sweetbreads
8 oz (225 g) button mushrooms
Stock
8 oz (225 g) puff pastry

Lightly grease an ovenproof dish.

Season the veal with the herbs, mace, salt and pepper.

Place in the dish.

Remove the rind from the bacon rashers and roll each one up.

Tuck the rolls between the cutlets.

Add the egg yolks or sweetbreads, and the mushrooms.

Pour over enough stock to cover.

Poll out the pastry to make a lid.

Bake in a moderate oven for 1 hour.

Oven: 350°F/180°C   Gas Mark 4

FORFAR BRIDIES

Serves 3-4

These are the Scottish equivalent of Cornish pasties, and are a specialty of Angus. Traditionally the pastry is made only of flour, salt and water, and no fat, but this makes it hard and tough on the outside. Rough puff or flaky pastry are good alternatives, though some Scottish cooks prefer to use shortcrusts or suet pastry.

1 lb (450 g) topside or rump steak
3 oz (75 g) shredded suet
1 onion, minced
Salt and pepper
1 lb (450 g) rough puff or flaky pastry

Beat the meat well with a rolling pin and cut into thin strips about 1 inch (2.5 cm) long.

Mix with the suet and minced onion.

Season well with salt and pepper.

Divide the pastry into three or four equal pieces.

On a floured board roll each piece into a round or oval shape.

Cover half of each round with a third or quarter of the beat mixture.

Brush the edges with water.

Fold over the other half of the pastry, press and crimp the edges.

Make a small hole in the top of each to allow the steam to escape.

Bake in a hot oven for 15 minutes, then reduce the temperatrure and bake for a further hour.

Serve hot, one per person.

Oven: 425°F/150°C Gas Mark 7

Reduce to: 350°F/180°C   Gas Mark 4

MUSSELBURGH PIE

Serves 6-8

Oysters used to be plentiful along the coast near Edinburgh, and this sumptuous pie was made with oysters wrapped up inside the meat. Thes days mussels are a cheap alternative.

3 lb (1.5 kg) mussels
1¹/² lbs (675 g) rump steak
1¹/² oz (40 g) beef suet
Seasoned flour
2 tablespoons oil
2 onions, finely chopped
1/2 pint (300 ml/ 1¹/⁴ cups) water
8 oz (225 g) puff pastry

Put the mussels in a pan of boiling salted water about 2 inches (5 cm) deep.

Cover with a lid and boil for 3 minutes.

Remove them from their shells.

Beat the steak until it is quite thin and cut into strips.

Place a few mussels and a piece of suet on each strip and roll up.

Dip each roll in seasoned flour and pack them into 2 pint (1 litre) pie dish round a pie funnel.

Heat the oil in a frying pan and cook the onions gently until golden brown.

Add the onions to the beef rolls in the pie dish.

Pour over the water.

Cover the dish with aluminium foil and cook in a moderate oven for 11/2-2 hours, or until the meat is tender.

Remove from the oven and leave to cool.

Roll out the pastry to make a lid.

Use the trimmings to decorate the pie.

Brush with milk or beaten egg to glaze.

Make a few holes in the top for the steam to escape

Bake in a hot oven for 30 minutes.

Oven: 350°F/180°C   Gas Mark 4

Increase to: 425°F/220°C   Gas Mark 7

STOVIES

Serves 4-6

This is a good way of using up left-over meat, poultry or game. the potatoes are stoved - that is, stewed in a pot on the cooker. Oatcakes and a glass of milk are the traditional accompaniements to this old Scots dish.

2 lb (900 g) potatoes
1 large onion
2 oz (50 g) butter, lard, or meat dripping
Salt and pepper
1/2 pint (300 ml/1¼ cups) stock
8 oz (225 g) left-over meat, poultry or game
Chopped parsley for garnishing

Peel and slice the potatoes and onion.

Melt the fat in a large, heavy saucepan.

Fry the onion lightly, then add the potatoes.

Season well with salt and pepper.

Pour over the stock. Bring to the boil.

Cover with a tight-fitting lid.

Simmer gently for 1 hour, stirring occasionally to prevent sticking.

Add the left-over meat and cook for a further 10 minutes.

Garnish with the parsley and serve hot.

CLAPSHOT

A traditional dish from the Orkney Islands, clapshot is often served with haggis.

1 lb (450 g) potatoes
1 lb (450 g) turnips
A handful of chives
1 oz (25 g) butter or dripping
A little salt and freshly ground black pepper

Peel the potatoes and cut them into even-sized pieces.

Cut the thick rind off the turnips and cut into even-sized pieces.

Put the prepared vegetables into a large saucepan and bring to the boil.

Cover and simmer for about 20 minutes until the vegetables are soft.

Drain off the water and shake the vegetables over a low heat to dry them out slightly.

Mash them and stir in the butter or dripping until it has melted.

Season with a little salt and freshly ground black pepper.

Wash and snip the chives with a pair of kitchen scissors and stir them into the mixture.

Serve hot.

SCOTCH EGGS

5 hard-boled eggs
Seasoned flour
1 lb (450 g) sausagemeat
1 beaten egg
Breadcrumbs
Oil for deep frying

Remove the shells from the hard-boiled eggs.

Dust the eggs with seasoned flour.

Divide the sausagemeat into 5 equal pieces.

On a floured surface flatten each piece into a oval shape large enough to cover an egg.

Place the egg in the centre and mould the sausagemeat round it, making sure the surface is free from cracks.

Coat each one in beaten egg.

Roll it in breadcrumbs, pressing the crumbs well in so that it is completely covered.

Heat the oil until it is really hot.

Carefully lower the Scotch eggs into the hot oil and cook for about 5-6 minutes, until brown all over.

Remove from the oil and drain well on kitchen paper.

Serve hot or cold.

POTTED HOUGH

Potting was a popular way of preserving meat, fish and game before the invention or refrigeration. This potted hough (shin of beef) is a tasty savoury dish for supper or high tea.

1 lb (450 g) hough (shin of beef)
A 2 lb (900 g) beef shin bone or knuckle of veal
1 level teaspoon salt
6 allspice berries
6 peppercorns
1 bay leaf

Put the meat and bone into a large saucepan and cover with cold water.

Bring to the boil and skim off any scum that rises to the surface.

Simmer for 3 to 4 hours until the meat is really tender.

Remove all meat from the bones and mince it.

Put into a wetted mould.

Return the bone to the saucepan and add the salt, allspice berries, peppercorns and bay leaf.

Boil rapidly until the liquid has reduced by half.

Pour over the stock over the meat in the mould.

Leave to set overnight.

When required, turn out the potted hough and serve with salad.

BASHED NEEPS

Neeps are large root vegetables known as swedes south of the border. In Scotland they are also referred to as turnips. This dish is tradtionaly served with haggis.

1 large swede or neep (about 2 lbs/1kg)
A large pinch of salt
2 oz (50 g) dripping or butter
Freshly ground black pepper
A handful of chives

Remove the rind from the swede.

Cut the vegetable into small pieces and put these inbto a saucepan of boiling water.

Add a large pinch of salt and bring to the boil.

Simmer with the lid on for about 15 to 20 minutes or until the swede is very soft.

Drain the swede and add the dripping or butter.

Mash the swede well and season with the ground pepper.

Turn into a serving dish.

Snip the chives into tiny pieces with a pair of scissors and sprinkle on top of the mashed neeps.

Serve immediately.

PAN HAGGERTY

1 lb (450 g) potatoes
2 medium onions
2 oz (50 g) dripping
4 oz (100 g) cheese
A littlke salt and pepper

Peel and slice the potatoes and onions.

Grate the cheese.

Melt the dripping in a large saucepan or deep frying pan.

Put in a layer of potatoes then onion then cheese and season with a little salt and pepper.

Repeat the layers until all the ingredients have been used.

Cover the pan and cook gently for about 45 minutes until the potatoes and onions are tender.

Remove the cover and place the pan under a hot grill to brown the cheese.

CHAPPIT TATTIES

Serves 6

This potato dish is traditionaly served with haggis.

1½ lbs (675 g) potatoes
2 oz (50 g) butter
4 tablespoons milk
A little salt and freshly ground black pepper

Peel the potatoes and cut into even-sized pieces.

Bring to the boil in a saucepan and simmer for about 20 minutes until soft.

Drain off the liquid and mash the potatoes.

Add the butter, milk, salt and pepper and beat well until the butter has melted and the potatoes are creamy.

Return the pan to the heat and cook gently stirring all the time to dry out the potatoes slightly.

Serve immediately.

KAILKENNY

Kailkenny was eaten as a main meal reather than as an accompaniment. Left-over kailkenny may be made into flat rouds and fried.

1 lb (450 g) potatoes
1 lb (450 g) cabbage
8 oz (225 g) carrots
2 tablespoons double cream
A little salt and freshly ground black pepper

Peel and dice the potatoes.

Scrape and slice the carrots.

Wash and shred the cabbage.

Cook the vegetables in water until soft

Mash the potatoes and carrots and mix with the cabbage.

Beat in the cream.

Season with a little salt and fresly ground black pepper.

Serve hot.

AYRSHIRE SWEET HAGGIS

Serves 6

Ayrshire is the area associated with the poet Robert Burns who was born in Alloway just south of Ayr. This dish is traditionally served on Saturday at high tea in the late afternoon. Any left over would be fried with rashers of Ayrshire bacon and served at breakfast the next day.

8 oz (225 g) medium oatmeal
4 oz (100 g) flour
8 oz (225 g) shredded suet
2 oz (50 g) soft brown sugar
2 oz (50 g) raisins
2 oz (50 g) currants
A little salt and pepper
Water

Put the oatmeal, flour, suet, sugar, raisins and currants into a bowl and mix well.

Season with a little salt and papper.

Add enough water to bind the mixture together without making it wet.

Turn into a greased 2 pint (1.15 litre) pudding basin.

Cover with greaseprooof paper and aluminium foil.

Put into a saucepan half full with boiling water.

Cover and steam for about 3 hours.

Serve hot.

Any left-overs may be sliced when cold and either fried or wrapped in aluminium foil and reheated in a moderate oven.

CROFTER'S PLUM PUDDING

Serves 4-6

This dish dates from around the end of the 19th century.

1 lb (450 g) flour
A pinch of salt
8 oz (225 g) shredded suet
8 oz (225 g) chopped raisins
1 large egg
About 1/2 pint (300 ml/1¹/⁴ cups) brown ale
1/2 teaspoon bicarbonate of soda

Sift the flour and salt into a large bowl.

Add the suet and raisins and mix well.

Beat the egg and add to the mixture.

Dissolve the bicarbonate of soda in a tablespoon of the ale and stir into the mixture.

Add enough of the remaining ale to make a stiff dropping consistency.

Turn the mixture into a greased 2 pint (1.15 litres) pudding basin.

Cover with a layer of greaseproof paper, then with a pudding cloth or piece of aluminium foil.

Place the basin in the upper part of a steamer or in a saucepan half full of boiling water.

Cover the steamer or saucepan with a tightly fitting lid and steam for about 3 hours.

Turn the pudding on to a hot dish and serve immediately.

CLOUTIE DUMPLING

This pudding is especially popular at Hogmanay and on birthdays. Coins wrapped in greaseproof paper are stirred into the mixture before it is cooked. Any left over can be fried for breakfast with bacon and egg. Cloutie or clootie is the name of the cloth in which the pudding is traditionaly cooked.

1 lb (450 g) self-raising flour
4 oz (100 g) shredded suet
4 oz (100 g) sugar
4 oz (100 g) currants
4 oz (100 g) raisins
1 teaspoon mixed spice
1 teaspoon cinnamon
1 large teaspoon treacle
Milk

Mix together the flour, suet, sugar, currants, raisins, mixed spice and the cinnamon.

Melt the treacle in a saucepan until runny.

Add the treacle to the dry ingredients.

Add enough milk to make a soft dough.

Put the mixture into a large damp cloth sprinkled generously with flour.

Tie the cloth around the dough loosely to allow the pudding to expand.

Put the pudding into a large saucepan of boiling water and steam for 2 hours.

Serve hot.

BRYDON TART

This dish from the Highlands may be served warm as a dessert with cream, or cold as a tea-time cake.

8 oz (225 g) self-raising flour
3 oz (75 g) butter
3 oz (75 g) lard
4 oz (100 g) caster sugar
1 teaspoon ground cinnamon
2 eggs
4 tablespoons apricot jam
Icing sugar for sprinkling

Sift the flour and rub in the butter and lard.

Add the sugar and ground cinnamon.

Beat the eggs and stir in the mixture to make a stiff dough.

Divide the dough into two equal-sized pieces.

Roll out each piece into an 8 inch (20 cm) circle.

Place one circle in the bottom of a greased 8 inch (20 cm) flan ring with a loose bottom.

Spread the apricot jam over the circle to within 1/2 inch (1 cm) of the edge.

Cover with the remaining circle of dough and seal the edges.

Bake for 30 minutes.

Turn out the tart and sprinkle with icing sugar.

Oven: 400°F/200°C   Gas Mark 6.

MORAYSHIRE APPLES

Serves 6

The old county of Morayshire is now part of the Grampian region and is known as the 'Garden of thre North'.

1¹/² lb (675 g) cooking apples
1/4 pint (150 ml/2/3 cup) water
4 oz (100 g) caster sugar
A pinch of ground cloves
3 oz (75 g) shredded suet
6 oz (175 g) medium oatmeal
2 oz (50 g) ground hazlenuts
4 oz (100 g) soft brown sugar

Put the caster sugar and the pinch of ground cloves into a small saucepan with the water.

Heat gently and stir until the sugar has dissolved.

Peel, core and slice the apples into a large pie dish.

Pour the sugared water over the apples.

Mix together the suet, oatmeal, hazlenuts and half of the brown sugar.

Sprinkle this mixture over the apples.

Sprinkle the remaining soft brown sugar over the top.

Bake for 45 to 50 minutes or until the top is browned.

Serve hot with cream.

Oven:350°F/180°C   Gas Mark 4

DRUMLANRIG PUDDING

Serves 6-8

This pudding is named after Drumlanrig Castle which was built around 1680 just north of Dumfries.

2 lbs (1 kg) rhubarb
6 oz (175 g) caster sugar
6 large slices of white bread
1 tablespoon water

Chop the rhubarb and put into a saucepan with the water and sugar.

Bring to the boil, cover and simmer very gently for about 15 minutes or until the rhubarb is soft.

Grease a 2 pint (1.15 litres) pudding basin or pie dish.

Put a layer of bread in the base.

Pour some rhubarb over the bread.

Add another layer of bread followed by some more rhubarb and continue adding layers until the dish is full, finishing with a layer of bread.

Cover with a pice of greaseproof paper and put a weight on top.

Leave the pudding in a cool place for at least 24 hours.

Loosen the pudding around the edges and turn out onto a serving plate.

Serve with cream.

TIPSY LAIRD

Serves 6

6 trifle sponges
3 tablespoons raspberry jam
3 oz (75 g) ratafia biscuits or macaroons
Grated rind of 1/2 lemon
1/4 pint (150 ml/2/3 cup) sherry
1 pint (600 ml/2½ cups) cold custard
1/4 pint (150 ml/2/3 cup) double cream
1 tablespoon Drambuie
Blanched flaked almonds to decorate

Split the trifle sponges in half lengthways.

Spread the halves with jam then sandwich them together and place them in a shallow dish.

Crumble the ratafia biscuits or macaroons and scatter them over the sponge.

Sprinkle the grated lemon rind on top.

Pour the sherry over the sponge and biscuits and leave for 1 hour.

Whisk the cold custard until creamy and spoon over the contents of the dish.

Whisk the cream and the Drambuie together until the mixture holds its shape.

Spread the flavoured cream over the custard.

Decorate with flaked almonds.

Serve chilled.

CRANNACHAN

This dessert is traditionaly served at harvest celebrations and at Hallowe'en. It is made using the traditional soft cheese called crowdie made in the Highlands.

2 oz (50 g) lightly toasted medium oatmeal
4 tablespoons malt whisky
3 tablespoons clear heather honey
4 oz (100 g) crowdie or cream cheese
8 oz (225 g) raspberries
1/4 pint (150 ml/2/3 cup) double cream

Mix the oatmeal, whisky and 1 tablespoon of the honey in a bowl, and leave for about 12 hours.

Stir in the cream cheese or crowdie and then the raspberries.

Whisk the cream until it holds its shape.

Put half of the cream into a dish or into individual glasses.

Spoon the oatmeal and cream cheese mixture over.

Cover with the remaining cream.

Pour the rest of the honey over the top.

Serve chilled.

FORTUNE TELLING CROWDIE

Serves 4

> 'A coin for wealth
> A ring for marriage
> A button for a bachelor
> A thimble for a spinster
> A whishbone for your heart's desire.'

Small silver charms were stirred into this dessert. Each charm had a special meaning. The dessert was eaten on the night of Hallowe'en and each guest would hope to find a favourable charm in his or her portion.

2 oz (50 g) lightly toasted oatmeal
1/2 pint (300 ml/1¼ cups) double cream
1 oz (25 g) caster sugar
1 tablespoon dark rum

Whip the cream until it holds its shape.

Stir in the sugar and rum and whisk again until thick.

Gently stir in the toasted oatmeal. Chill well.

CALEDONIAN CREAM

Serves 4-6

2 tablespoons Dundee Marmelade
2 tablespoons brandy or whisky
Juice of 1/2 lemon
1/2 pint (300 ml/1¼ cups) double cream
1 oz (25 g) caster sugar

Put the marmelade, sugar and the leamon juice inbto a saucepan and heat gently until the sugar has dissolved.

Remove from the heat and allow to cool.

Transfer the mixture to a bowl and add the cream and the brandy or whisky.

Whisk the mixture until thick.

Spoon the cream into individual glasses and chill.

LOTHIAN GINGERBREAD

8 oz (225 g) flour
1 teaspoon bicarbonate of soda
2 teaspoons ground ginger
1 teaspoon ground cinnamon
A pinch of salt
6 oz (175 g) butter
6 oz (175 g) treacle
4 oz (100 g) soft brown sugar
6 tablespoons milk
2 eggs
2 oz (50 g) sultanas
2 oz (50 g) chopped walnuts

Place the butter, treacle and sugar into a saucepan and heat gently until well combined.

Remove from the heat and stir in the milk and eggs.

Sift the flour, salt, ginger, cinnamon and bicarbonate of soda together.

Make a well in the centre and gradually beat in the treacle mixture until the batter is smooth.

Stir in the sultanas and chopped walnuts.

Pour into a greased and lined 2 lb (1 kg) loaf tin.

Bake for 1$^{1/4}$ hours.

Oven: 325°F/160°C   Gas Mark 3

SCOTTISH BLACK BUN

'Bun' is an old Scottish word for a fruity cake which is eaten at Hogmanay. It was originally baked enclosed in bread dough to retain the moisture and flavour, but it is now more commonly encased in a pastry dough. The case was discarded before the cake was eaten. As with all good fruit cakes it is at its best at least 2 weeks after it is made. It should be kept wrapped in greaseproof paper and aluminium foil in an airtight tin.

For the pastry case:
8 oz (225 g) flour
1 teaspoon bicarbonate of soda
A pinch of salt
2 oz (50 g) butter
2 oz (50 g) lard

For the cake:
8 oz (225 g) flour
3 teaspoons allspice
1 teaspoon bicarbonate of soda
1 teaspoon cream of tartar
4 oz (100 g) brown sugar
12 oz (375 g) currants
12 oz (375 g) raisins
4 oz (100 g) ground almonds
2 oz (50 g) chopped mixed candied peel
2 tablespoons brandy
1/4 pint (150 ml/2/3 cup) milk
1 beaten egg

To make the pastry case:

Sift the flour, salt and bicarbonate of soda into a bowl.

Rub in the butter and lard until the mixture resembles breadcrumbs.

Add enough cold water to make a soft dough.

Leave the dough to rest for 30 minutes.

Roll out 2/3 of the dough to line a greased and lined 8 inch (20 cm) cake tin.

To make the cake:

Sift together the flour, allspice, bicarbonate of soda and the cream of tartar.

Add the sugar, currants, raisins, ground almonds and the chopped mixed candied peel.

Pour in the brandy and the milk and mix well.

Turn the mixture into the prepared pastry dough case.

Turn over the top edge of the dough and moisten the edges with water.

Roll out the remaining pastry dough and place over the cake mixture pressing the edges of the dough together securely.

Brush with beaten egg.

Plunge a skewer right trough the pastry case and the cake four times.

Cover the top with greaseproof paper.

Bake for 30 minutes then lower the oven temperature and bake for a further 2 hours.

Oven: 400°F/200°C   Gas Mark 6

Reduce to: 325°F/160°C   Gas Mark 3

DUNDEE CAKE

Popular in the 19th century in Dundee this cake became famous throughout the country. It should be covered with whole almonds.

10 oz (275 g) self-raising flour
A teaspoon mixed spice
A pinch of salt
8 oz (225 g) butter
8 oz (225 g) caster sugar
5 eggs
Grated rind of 1 lemon
2 oz (50 g) ground almonds
6 oz (175 g) raisins
6 oz (175 g) sultanas
6 oz (175 g) currants
2 oz (50 g) chopped mixed peel
3 oz (75 g) blanched whole almonds
1 tablespoon brandy
A littke milk to mix

Cream the butter and sugar together until light and fluffy

Gradually beat in the eggs one at the time with a little of the flour to prevent the mixture from curdling.

Sift in the remaining flour, salt, ground almonds and the mixed spice stirring gently.

Stir in the grated lemon rind, the raisins, currants, sultanas and the mixed peel.

Stir in the brandy and enough of the milk to make a fairly soft dropping consistency.

Turn into a greased and lined 8 inch (20 cm) cake tin.

Smooth the top with a palette knife and arrange the almonds to cover the surface of the mixture.

Place a circle of greaseproof papaer on top of the cake and leave it to rest for a couple of hours. This helps to prevent the dried fruit from sinking.

Bake in the centre of the oven for 3 hours.

Remove from the oven but leave the cake in the tin for at least 20 minutes before turning out, then cool on a wire rack.

Keep for at least 2 weeks in an airtight tin before using.

Oven: 325°F/160°C   Gas Mark 3

ANGUS FRUITCAKE

1 lb (450 g) flour
1 lb (450 g) cooking apples
2 tablespoons golden syrup or honey
6 oz (175 g) butter
2 teaspoons mixed spice
2 teaspoons bicarbonate of soda
1 egg
1/2 pint (300 ml/1$^{1/4}$ cups) buttermilk

Put the golden syrup or honey into a saucepan

Peel, core and slice the apples and add to the syrup or honey.

Cover and simmer for about 10 to 15 minutes until the apples are soft. Leave to cool.

Sift the flour, mixed spice and bicarbonate of soda into a bowl. Rub in the butter.

Beat the egg and buttermilk together and gradually add to the flour. Stir in the apples and syrup.

Mix well to make a soft dropping consistency.

Turn into a greased and lined 7 inch (18 cm) cake tin.

Bake for 1$^{1/2}$ hours.

Oven: 350°F/180°C   Gas Mark 4

SELKIRK BANNOCK

This rich fruit bread is said to have been enjoyed by Queen Victoria. It was first made in Selkirk in south-eastern Scotland around the mid-19th century.

1 lb (450 g) strong plain flour
1 oz (25 g) fresh yeast
4 oz (100 g) caster sugar
7 fl oz (200 ml/3/4 cup) warm milk
1 teaspoon salt
2 oz (250 g) lard
2 oz (50 g) butter
8 oz (225 g) sultanas
1 beaten egg
A little extra caster sugar for glazing

Crumble the yeast into the warm milk and add a teaspoon of the sugar. Stir until the sugar has dissolved and leave for 15 minutes or until frothy.

Sift the flour into a bowl and add the salt.

Rub in the butter and lard.

Add the remaining sugar.

Gradually add the yeast liquid to the mixture to make a fairly soft dough.

Knead on a floured surface for 10 minutes until smooth and elastic.

Put the dough into a bowl, cover with a damp cloth and leave in a warm place until doubled in size.

Knock back the dough and knead in the sultanas and the sugar.

Shape into 2 small rounds or 2 large round and place on a greased baking sheet.

Leave in a warm place for about 30 minutes to prove.

Bake for 30 minutes then remove the bannocks from the oven.

Glaze the top with beaten egg and sprinkle with a little caster sugar.

Return to the oven for a further 20 to 30 minutes.

Cool on a wire rack.

Serve, thinly sliced, and spread with butter.

Oven: 350°F/180°C   Gas Mark 4

ORKNEY BROONIE

This delicious cake is rather like a rich gingerbread. It should be made at least a week before it is needed since it is better when left to mature.

8 oz (225 g) fine oatmeal
4 oz (100 g) self-raising flour
4 oz (100 g) butter
A pinch of salt
4 oz (100 g) soft brown sugar
2 teaspoons ground ginger
1 teaspoon bicarbonate of soda
2 oz (50 g) treacle
4 oz (100 g) golden syrup
1 egg
1/4 pint (150 ml/2/3 cup) buttermilk

Mix the oatmeal and flour in a bowl and rub in the butter.

Add the salt, sugar, ginger and bicarbonate of soda.

Stir in the treacle and golden syrup.

Beat the egg and buttermilk together and add to the mixture.

Grease and line an 8 inch (20 cm) square tin and pour the mixture into the tin.

Bake for 30 to 40 minutes.

Oven: 350°F/180°C   Gas Mark 4

PETTICOAT TAILS

This thin, crisp and shaped shortbread is a specialty of Edinburgh. There is some controversy over the origin of its name. Some sources say that it takes its shape and is named after the bell-hoop petticoats worn by fashionable ladies in the 19th century. Others say the name is more likely to be a corruption of the French name for little cakes - petites gatelles'.

8 oz (225 g) flour
2 oz (50 g) rice flour
4 oz (100 g) butter
1 oz (25 g) lard
A little milk to mix
2 oz (50 g) caster sugar
1 teaspoon caraway seeds
Caster sugar for sprinkling

Sift the flour and the rice flour together.

Add the sugar and caraway seeds.

Rub in the butter and lard.

Add enough milk to make a firm dough.

Knead gently on a floured surface.

Roll out to a thickness of about 1/4 inch (5 mm).

Cut out a large circle the size of a dinner plate.

Cut out a small circle about 4 inches (10 cm) in diameter in the middle.

Crimp the outer edges with a finger and thumb.

Cut the outer ring into 8 segments or petticoat tails.

Prick each segment 2 or 3 times with a fork and place them on a greased baking sheet.

Bake for 20 to 25 minutes or until golden brown.

Remove from the oven and sprinkle with caster sugar.

Leave the petticoat tails to cool then reassemble the pattern on a large plate or tray.

Oven: 350°F/180°C   Gas Mark 4

AYRSHIRE SHORTBREAD

Unlike other shortbreads, this shortbread is made with cream.

6 oz (175 g) flour
2 oz (50 g) rice flour or ground rice
4 oz (100 g) butter
3 oz (75 g) caster sugar
1 egg yolk
2 tablespoons cream

Sift the flour into a bowl and add the rice flour or ground rice and sugar.

Rub in the butter.

Beat the egg yolk and the cream together and add to the mixture.

Work the mixture into a dough and knead this lightly on a floured surface until smooth.

Roll out the dough to a thickness of about 1/4 inch (5 mm). Cut out circles with a small pastry cutter.

Place the circles on a greased baking sheet.

Bake for 15 minutes.

Oven: 350°F/180°C   Gas Mark 4

SCONES

Scones probably originated from the Dutch 'Schoonbrot', a kind of square cake made in the 16th century. They were traditionaly cooked on an iron girdle which was rubbed with salt and not greased. To make the best scones, handle as little as possible and make as quickly as possible.

GIRDLE SCONES

8 oz (225 g) flour
1 teaspoon bicarbonate of soda
1/2 teaspoon cream of tartar
A pinch of salt
1/2 oz (15 g) caster sugar
1/4 pint (150 ml/2/3 cup) buttermilk

Pre-heat the girdle or a lightly greased frying pan.

Sift the flour, bicarbonate of soda, cream of tartar and salt into a bowl.

Add the sugar and mix well.

Add enough buttermilk to make a fairly stiff dough.

Knead lightly on a floured board until smooth.

Roll out the dough to make a circle of about 1/2 inch (1 cm) thick.

Cut the circle into quarters.

Cook the quarters on a hot girdle for about 10 minutes on each side or until risen and beginning to brown.

Wrap in a clean cloth and cool on a rack.

BRIDE'S BONN

This is a recipe from the Shetland Islands and is also known as Bride's Bun and Bridal Cake. The cake was traditionaly made on the wedding day by the bride's mother who then held it over her daughter's head and broke it as the bride entered her new home as a married woman. The bride and bridegroom had to eat all the pieces of the cake to ensure a happy marriage.

5 oz (150 g) self-raising flour
1 teaspoon baking powder
2 oz (50 g) butter
1 oz (25 g) caster sugar
1/2 teaspoon caraway seeds
A little milk to mix

Sift the flour and the baking powder into a bowl and rub in the butter.

Stir in the sugar and caraway seeds.

Add enough milk to make a stiff dough.

Knead the dough lightly on a floured board and roll out into a round about 1/2 inch (1 cm) thick.

Cut the round into quarters.

Bake on a hot girdle for 5 to 10 minutes on each side.

These are best served the same day.

OATCAKES

True oatcakes are made using no flour. They were originally baked on a hot girdle. They can be fairly tricky to make. The secret is to make only enough dough for one baking and to roll out the mixture while the water is still hot.

4 oz (100 g) medium oatmeal
A pinch of salt
1/2 teaspoon bicarbonate of soda
1/2 oz (15 g) dripping or lard
3 tablespoons hot water
Extra medium oatmeal for rolling

Mix the salt and bicarbonate of soda with the oatmeal.

Rub in the fat.

Add 3 tablespoons of very hot water.

Mix quickly to make a slightly sticky dough.

Roll out the dough very thinly on a surface lightly sprinkled with oatmeal.

Cut out circles with a pastry cutter.

Put the oatcakes on to a greased baking sheet and rub them with oatmeal.

Bake for 20 minutes.

Turn each oatcake over with a palette knife and bake for a further 10 minutes.

Cool on a wire rack and store in an airtight tin.

Serve warm either by toasting lightly or heating in a low oven.

Oven: 350°F/180°C   Gas Mark 4

FIFE BANNOCKS

Bannocks are baked on a girdle and are thicker and heavier than oatcakes. They are made all over Scotland and the choice of ingredients reflect the type of grain grown locally. In Fife, wheat is the staple grain.

6 oz (175 g) flour
1/2 oz (15 g) butter
4 oz (100 g) fine oatmeal
1 teaspoon bicarbonate of soda
1 teaspoon cream of tartar
1/2 oz (15 g) caster sugar
A pinch of salt
1/4 pint (150 ml/2/3 cup) buttermilk

Sift the flour, salt, bicarbonate of soda and cream of tartar into a bowl.

Rub in the butter.

Stir in the oatmeal and sugar.

Add enough buttermilk to make a stiff dough.

Knead lightly on a floured surface until smooth.

Roll out into a round about 1/2 inch (1 cm) thick.

Divide the round into 8 and cook on a hot girdle for about 5 to 10 minutes on each side.

Serve warm.

DROPPED SCONES

'Scone' is derived fom the Gaelic word 'sgonn' and is pronounced 'skon'.

4 oz (100 g) flour
1 teaspoon bicarbonate of soda
1 teaspoon cream of tartar
A pinch of salt
1 oz (25 g) caster sugar
1 egg
1/4 pint (150 ml/2/3 cup) milk

Sift the flour, bicarbonate of soda, cream of tartar and salt into a bowl.

Stir in the sugar.

Beat the egg and milk together and gradually add to the dry ingredients stirring all the time to prevent any lumps forming.

Put tablespoonful of the batter on to a hot girdle or lightly greased frying pan.

Cook until bubbles appear on the surface of each pancake and the underside is golden brown.

Turn each pancake over with a palette knife and cook the other side until golden.

Serve warm with butter.

SCOTTISH BAPS

1 oz (25 g) fresh yeast
1 teaspoon caster sugar
1/4 pint (150 ml/2/3 cup) water water
1/4 pint (150 ml/2/3 cup) milk
1 lb (450 g) strong plain flour
2 teaspoon salt
2 oz (50 g) butter

Dissolve the sugar in the water which should be hand hot.

Crumble in the yeast, stir then leave for about 15 minutes or until frothy.

Sift the flour and salt into a bowl.

Rub in the butter.

Gradually add the yeast mixture.

Add enough of the milk to make a soft dough that is not too sticky.

Turn the dough out on to a floured board and knead for about 10 minutes until it is smooth and elastic.

Put the dough into a bowl and cover with a clean damp cloth.

Leave in a warm place until the dough has dubbled in size.

Knock back and kned again.

Divide the mixture into 8 or 10 pieces and shape each piece into a flattish round.

Place the baps on greased baking sheets, cover with a clean cloth and leave to rise in a warm place.

Sprinkle the baps with a little flour and bake for 15 to 20 minutes.

Oven: 400°F/200°C   Gas Mark 6

PORRIDGE

Porridge is one of the best known Scottish specialities. Usually eaten for breakfast, it is filling and makes a good start to the day especially when about to spend a long day in the hills. It is said that porridge should be eaten standing up.

1 pint (600 ml/2$^{1/2}$ cups) water
2$^{1/2}$ oz (65 g) medium oatmeal
A pinch of salt

Put the water into a saucepan and bring to the boil.

Add the oatmeal while stirring to prevent any lumps forming.

Cover and simmer gently for about 15 minutes.

Add the salt and stir it in well.

Cover the pan again and simmer for a further 10 minutes or until the porridge is fairly thick.

Porridge is traditionaly served hot with separate bowls of cream or milk. Each spoonful of porridge is dipped into the cream or milk and then eaten.

DUNDEE MARMELADE

Makes about 6 lbs
(2.75 kg)

Dundee is famous for its marmalade. It began as a preserve made from quinces and takes its name from the Portuguese word for quince - 'marmelo'. Seville oranges in the preserve were substituted for the quinces and this new preserve quickly gained in popularity.

2 lbs (1 kg) Seville oranges
Juice and pips of 3 lemons
4 pints (2.25 litres/10 cups) water
4 lbs (1.75 kg) sugar

Wash the oranges thoroughly and cut into thin slices.

Put the slices into a large preserving pan with the water.

Bring to the boil and boil for about 1 hour.

Remove fom the heat and allow to cool enough to be able to handle the oranges.

Remove the fruit and cut the rind into thin strips.

Remove the pips and put into a muslin bag with the pips from the lemons.

Return the orange pulp, the rind and the pips in the muslin bag to the preserving pan.

Add the lemon juice.

Bring to the boil again and boil rapidly for 15 minutes.

Remove the muslin bag of pips.

Warm the sugar and add to the mixture in the pan.

Stir over a low heat until the sugar has dissolved.

Bring to the boil and boil rapidly until setting point has been reached. This will be at 220°F/105°C when measured with a sugar thermometer. The mixture should set when a little is put on a cold saucer.

Leave the marmalade to cool a little then pour into hot, sterilised jars and seal.

TABLET

Tablet is another name for the fudge made in the Scottish Lowlands.

1/2 pint (300 ml/1¹/⁴ cups) milk
1 lb (450 g) granulated sugar
4 oz (100 g) butter
A few droips of vanilla essence

Put the milk and sugar into a large saucepan and heat gently until the sugar has dissolved.

Bring to the boil and boil rapidly until the mixture forms a soft ball when a little is dropped into cold water. This should take about 20 minutes.

Remove from the heat and add the butter and a few drops of vanilla essence.

Beat the mixture until the butter has melted and the mixture begins to set.

Pour into a greased and lined 7 inch (18 cm) square tin and leave to cool.

Cut into squares when cool and store in an airtight tin.

GLASGOW TOFFEE

Glaswegians were fond of making sweets in the 18th and 19th centuries as sugar was ready available, imported from the West Indies. The women who made these sweets and then sold them on th streets were named 'Sweety Wives'.

4 oz (100 g) butter
8 oz (225 g) sugar
1/4 pint (150 ml/2/3 cup) milk
6 oz (175 g) golden syrup
2 oz (50 g) plain chocolate
A few driops of vanilla essence

Melt the butter in a saucepan.

Add the sugar, milk, golden syrup and pieces of chocolate.

Stir the mixture over a low heat until the sugar and syrup have dissolved.

Bring to the boil and boil rapidly, until the point when the toffee will harden when a little is put into a cup of cold water. The temperature should reach 250°F/120°C.

Take off the heat and leave for a few minutes to cool slightly.

Beat in the vanilla essence and pour the toffee into a greased shallow tin.

Leave until the toffee has almost set then cut into squares.

The toffee should be wrapped in wax paper and kept in an airtight tin.

EDINBURGH ROCK

This is a well-known confection thought to have been first made by a young man called Sandy Ferguson who enjoyed making sweets in his own home. His sweets were so popular with his friends that he decided to go to Edinburgh to start making them on a larger scale. The rock is still made in Edinburgh from the original recipe.

1 lb (450 g) granulated sugar
7 fl oz (200 ml/3/4 cup) water
1/2 teaspoon cream of tartar
Colouring and flavouring as desired
Icing sugar

Dissolve the sugar in the water over a low heat.

Add the cream of tartar.

Bring to the boil and boil rapidly until the temperature reaches 260°F/130°C or until the mixture forms a hard ball when a little is dropped into cold water.

Remove from the heat and stir in any flavouring and colouring.

When the mixture is cool enough to handle pour it on to an oiled surface.

Turn the edges of the mixture into the centre with an oiled knife.

When it becomes firm enough, sprinkle icing sugar over and pull the mixture up with your hands then let it drop down again. Continue in this way until the mixture hardens.

Pull into one long length about 1/2 inch (1 cm) thick then cut into shorter lengths.

Put these on tray dusted with icing sugar and sprinkle more icing sugar over the rock.

Leave in a warm place until the rock becomes powdery and crumbly. This may take anything from 1 to 7 days.

Store in an airtight tin.

WHIPKULL

Also known as Whipcol, this drink is traditionaly served at Christmas breakfast in the Shetland Islands, a custom shared with the Norwegians.

4 oz (100 g) caster sugar
4 egg yolks
2 fl oz (3 tablespoons/1/4 cup) rum

Put the sugar and the egg yolks in the top of a double boiler.

Beat over boiling water until the mixture is thick and creamy and the whisk leaves a trail.

Gradually add the rum, beating all the time.

Whisk for a further 5-10 minutes then pour into glasses.

This drink may be served hot or chilled and is especially good accompanied by rich shortbread.

ATHOLL BROSE

This creamy drink is named after the Duke of Atholl who lived in the 15th century and is believed to have enjoyed it. It is served on St.Andrew's Day and at Hogmanay.

2 oz (50 g) fine oatmeal
2 tablespoons clear heather honey
1/4 pint (150 ml/2/3 cup) Scotch Whisky
1/2 pint (300 ml/1¹/⁴ cups) water
1/4 pint (150 ml/2/3 cup) single cream
1 teaspoon lemon juice

Mix the oatmeal and the water together, stir and leave for at least 1 hour.

Strain the liquid and discard the oatmeal.

Stir the honey into the liquid and heat gently until the honey has dissolved.

Remove from the heat and stir in the whisky and lemon juice.

Add the cream and whisk lightly to blend well.

Chill until needed.

SCOTTISH MILK

Serves 4

2 eggs
1/2 pint (300 ml/1¼ cups) milk
2 oz (50 g) caster sugar
4 tablespoons Scotch whisky
A little grated nutmeg

Separate the yolks of the eggs from the whites.

Beat the egg yolks with the sugar until thick.

Add the milk and whisky and whisk well.

Whisk the egg whites until stif but not dry and fold into the drink.

Sprinkle with a little grated nutmeg.

Serve in chilled glasses.

THE COUNTRY RECIPE SERIES

Titles already published in this Series

Kent
Sussex
Yorkshire
Scottish

Other titles to be published in this Series include

Cambridgeshire
Cornwall
Cumberland & Westmorland
Cumbria
Derbyshire
Devon
Dorset
English
Essex
Gloucestershire
Hampshire
Hereford & Worcestershire
Irish
Lancashire
Leicestershire
Norfolk
Northumberland & Durham
Oxfordshire
Somerset
Suffolk
Warwickshire
Welsh
Wiltshire

The titles already published are available throughout the UK but
any difficulty in obtaining a copy or any correspondence relating
to a title should be addressed to County Publications, Suite 1
Royal Star Arcade, High Street, Maidstone, Kent, ME14 5EG.
Tele: 01622 764 555 Fax: 01622 763 197